Boxing Kangaroo

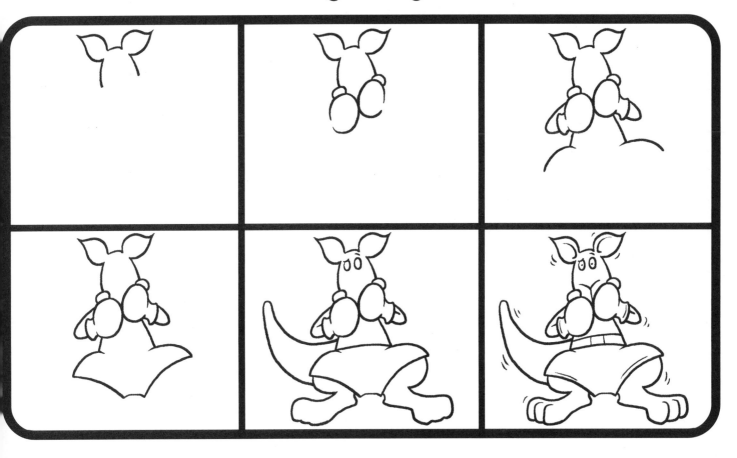

caveman

Bendy Girl

Gangster

Rude Girl   Chef

Cup Winner

Skateboarder

Wise Owl

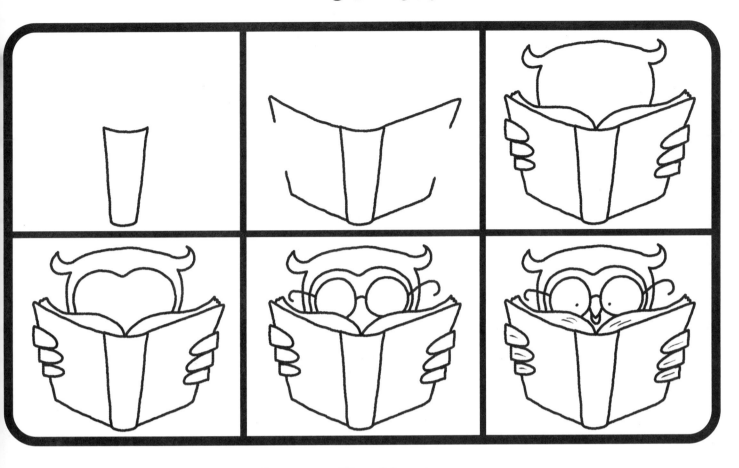

Hippo Ballerina

Penguin Waiter

Sneaky Snake

American Footballer

Clown

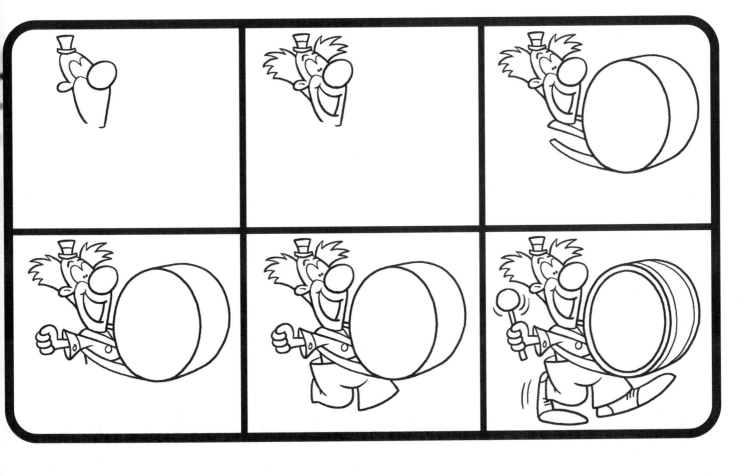

cycling Gorilla

Dancing Pharaoh

Sweeping Girl

Cool Cat

Hula Girl

Big Builder

Angry Man

Daft Dog

Karate Girl   Scarecrow

Artist

Canoeing Moose

Tourist

Parachuting

Dinghy Ride

Dinner Bear

Screaming Girl

Tarzan the Tiger

Diver

Wet Dog

Deep Sea Diver

Party Girl

Easter Bunny

Fat Bat

Snowman

Idea boy

Ghost

Flying Pig

Princess   footballer

fisherman

Ice-hockey Player

Thin Weightlifter

Jester

Kite Flying

Rhino on a Bike

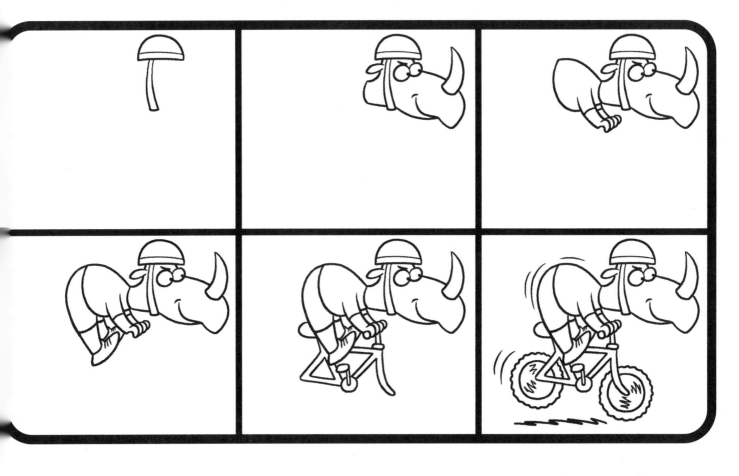

Shy Girl

Surgeon

Body Builder

old Man

freezing

Yo-yo Boy

Skating Bear

Reindeer

Crying Baby   Duck Spy

Knight on Horseback

Rock Drummer

Hiker

Space-hopper Girl

Teddy cuddle

Elephant Tightrope

Hungry cat

Basketball Player

Surfing Shark

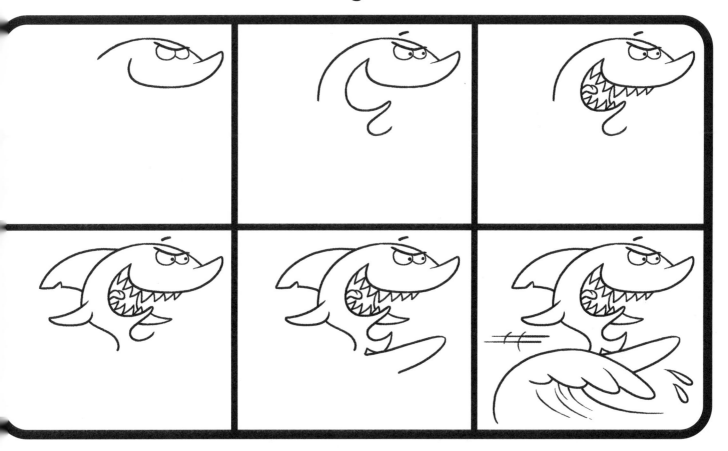

Speedy Snail

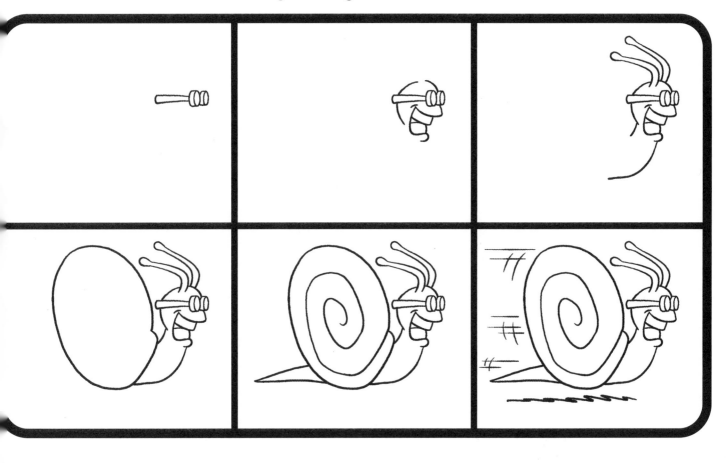

Keep-fit ostrich

Painter

Frog Swimmer

Rock Star

Boy Scout

Pirate

Computer and Mouse

Tortoise

cowboy

In Love

Viking

Wizard

Scientist

Witch

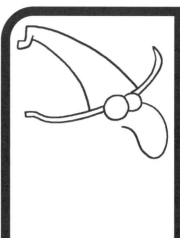

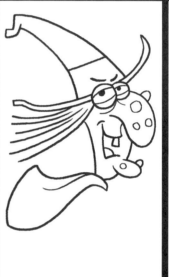

Goldfish Rave

Burglar

Santa

Cheeky Chicken

Champion

Little Angel

Little Devil

Busy Beaver

Queen

Punky Parrot

Bookworm

Sheila Sheep

Cool Banana

Silly Spider

Mobile Phone

Hippy Hamster

Sherlock Bones